Spend Half a Day in East Aurora

DATES IN THE STATES

A COUPLE TRAVELING THE UNITED
STATES ON A BUDGET

I0541626

Mystery Date
East Aurora, NY

By Dates in the States

![Street view of Vidler's 5 & 10 store in East Aurora, NY with a red and white striped awning and a street clock]

"Our passion is travel, and we want to share our adventures to inspire others to explore the world with their loved ones. Dare to live beyond the box."

Dates in the States

Introduction

Hey there! We're Crystal and Shane, the duo behind Dates in the States, where we share our love for discovering unique adventures, unforgettable moments, and hidden gems across the U.S. Whether you're searching for a fun date idea, a new place to explore, or just a little inspiration, we've got you covered!

Our Mystery Date Books are designed to help couples (and adventurous friends!) shake up their routine and experience the best local spots in a fun, intentional way. Inside, you'll find a curated collection of date ideas—each one meant to be completed over the course of a single day in a specific neighborhood. All of which are a surprise until you flip the page!

We hope this book helps you laugh more, explore more, and connect more—with each other and with your city. Let the mystery begin!

Here's What To Expect:

Ready to fall in love with a town that feels like it's straight out of a storybook? This Mystery Date Book is your ticket to a day of charm, flavor, and unforgettable memories in East Aurora, NY — a hidden gem just outside of Buffalo.

Inside this Mystery Date Book, you'll start with a scenic hike to a hidden waterfall, followed by a delicious, flavor-packed meal at a local favorite. Then, take your time exploring Main Street, where one-of-a-kind shops and nostalgic finds line the sidewalks. End your adventure with a cozy movie night at a restored vintage theater, complete with gourmet popcorn made in-house.

Whether you're planning a romantic day trip, a fun outing with friends, or just need an excuse to explore somewhere new, this East Aurora edition will help you rediscover the magic of a day well spent.

Start

Eternal Flame Falls
Orchard Park, NY

Kick off your mystery date with a scenic hike to Eternal Flame Falls, tucked away in Chestnut Ridge Park. This moderate, 1.5-mile round-trip hike leads you through scenic woodlands, across small creek crossings, and down a few rocky sections before revealing a mesmerizing sight—a waterfall with a flickering flame inside!

This little part of the waterfall rock emits natural gas which is the cause for this flame. It's always lit, but in the case that it's not - you can light it with a match and it will come alive again.

Use the Seufert Road parking lot, located at the southern entrance of the park. Follow the Eternal Flame Trailhead signs to begin your hike. We suggest starting your hike around 2pm in order to stay on schedule to complete the next couple stops on your date!

Second Stop

Arriba Tortilla

40 Riley St.

East Aurora, NY 14052

After your hike, it's time to head into downtown East Aurora for an early dinner at Arriba Tortilla around 4:00 PM. This lively, locally loved Mexican eatery is known for its bold flavors, fresh ingredients, and laid-back atmosphere, making it the perfect spot to relax and refuel.

Whether you're craving street-style tacos, massive burritos, sizzling fajitas, or their famous Mexican street corn, there's something on the menu to satisfy every craving. Pair your meal with a refreshing house-made margarita—the perfect way to toast to a great start to your date. (Don't worry, you'll have plenty of time to walk it off as you explore Main Street afterward!)

Third Stop

Vidler's 5 & 10

676 - 694 Main St.

East Aurora, NY 14052

Before your final stop of the evening, you'll likely have some time to kill—so why not take a leisurely stroll down Main Street to walk off that delicious meal (and those margaritas)?

Downtown East Aurora is full of small-town charm, lined with locally owned shops, cozy cafés, and historic buildings that make for a picturesque and relaxing walk. The inviting atmosphere makes it easy to slow down, window-shop, and enjoy each other's company.

One stop you absolutely can't miss is the legendary Vidler's 5 & 10. Established in 1930, this iconic variety store has been a staple of East Aurora for nearly a century. Spanning four connected buildings and over 75,000 quirky items, Vidler's is a true treasure trove of nostalgia —filled with old-fashioned candy, retro toys, unique gifts, kitchen gadgets, and vintage-style souvenirs.

Fourth Stop

Aurora Theatre & Popcorn Shop

673 Main St.

East Aurora, NY 14052

Spoiler alert: Your final stop is a classic movie night at the beloved Aurora Theatre—but first, you'll need the perfect snack.

Just next door, The Popcorn Shop offers a mouthwatering variety of gourmet popcorn, from sweet to savory and everything in between.

Swing by before the show to grab a bag (or two!) and elevate your movie night the East Aurora way.

Final Stop

Aurora Theatre

673 Main St.

East Aurora, NY 14052

End your night with a 7pm showing of a movie at the historic Aurora Theatre, a beautifully restored cinema with a classic marquee and old-time charm. Built in 1925, this theater has kept the spirit of vintage movie-going alive, offering a cozy and romantic setting to enjoy a film together. Whether it's a classic favorite or a new release, you'll love the intimate atmosphere and nostalgic feel.

If you visit around the holidays, you may even have the chance to watch a Christmas movie that was actually filmed in East Aurora!

Add Your Photos

Keepsakes

Thank you for joining us on this mystery date adventure! We hope you've enjoyed the delightful experiences and memorable moments we've crafted just for you in East Aurora, NY.

But the adventure doesn't stop here! Keep exploring exciting mystery dates in other cities and uncover new romantic experiences across the U.S. by visiting our website, DatesInTheStates.com. There, you can purchase both physical copies and digital downloads of our mystery date books. Plus, don't miss out on our Mystery Date Book Club, where you can receive a brand-new mystery date book every month!

Tag us in your date photos on social media! @datesinthestates

Check out some of our other Mystery Date Books:

Webster, NY – Lakeside charm, local eats, and small-town surprises erfect for a relaxing day out.

Haunted Irondequoit, NY – Explore the eerie side of town with this hilling look into the most haunted businesses and their spine-ngling stories.

Hornell, NY – A hidden gem in the Finger Lakes region with art, ature, and charming local spots waiting to be discovered.

Love ROC + Cats – Explore local art, sip coffee with adoptable cats, rowse a charming bookstore, and end with a delicious downtown heal. Perfect for solo dates, friend hangouts, or cat-loving couples!

✖ Shop them all at DatesInTheStates.com
📷 Tag your adventures: @datesinthestates

our next date is only a page away.

About the Creators

Crystal, the writer and creator, is a storyteller at heart. When she's not uncovering hidden gems for the next date night idea, she runs her own digital marketing company, helping small businesses improve their content marketing, increase visibility in their communities, and streamline their online presence.
Visit: crystalstatskey.com

Shane, her husband and partner in adventure, is a dedicated personal trainer and the owner of Beekstar Fitness in Irondequoit, NY. He specializes in working with clients who have limited mobility, helping them build muscle and focus on pain areas so they can regain strength and confidence in their daily lives.
Visit: beekstarfitness.com

Crystal and Shane have explored every U.S. state except Alaska (coming soon!) and are now visiting countries in alphabetical order. Whether road-tripping or curating Mystery Date experiences, they're always chasing their next adventure.

Local Love

A few local gems in East Aurora worth exploring on your next date.

EAST AURORA CO-OP MARKET
COZY CO-OP GROCERY W/ LOCAL GOODS
591 MAIN ST, EAST AURORA, NY 14052

42 NORTH BREWING COMPANY
LAID-BACK BREWERY WITH CRAFT BEERS
25 PINE ST, EAST AURORA, NY 14052

ELM STREET BAKERY
AMAZING WOOD-FIRED PIZZAS
72 ELM ST, EAST AURORA, NY 14052

Want to see your business here? See the next page for details on how to join!

Want to be featured?

MYSTERY DATE BOOK PACKAGES

—

Are you a small business looking to reach new customers? Feature your business in our next Mystery Date Book! Choose from our partnership packages below to connect with couples seeking unique experiences and exclusive deals.

Package One

LOCAL LOVE LISTING

—

A quick shoutout to show you're part of the neighborhood vibe.

Listed in the "Local Love" section of your designated neighborhood date book

Includes business name, address, and social link

Optional: Offer a small promo (e.g., 10% off for book holders)

1 social media shout-out when the book launches

$45

Package Two

FEATURE STOP

—

You're not just a business— you're part of the experience.

Marked as a "Must-Stop" on a Mystery Date

Full-page feature in the book with your story, offerings and photo

Includes 1 social media feature — a dedicated post and story highlighting your business

Note: To ensure each feature is genuine and experience-based, we require a hosted visit prior to inclusion.

$95

Package Three

PARTNER & SELLER

—

Be the spot and the source.

Everything in Tier 2

PLUS: Option to sell the Mystery Date Books at your location

Includes a bulk purchase of 10 books (yours to price + sell)

Keep 100% of the profits from in-store sales

Bonus: Tag as an official pickup location in our promotions

$150

Prices are subject to change

Feel free to reach us at any time by sending us an email to say hi and to learn more! We look forward to hearing from you.

| www.datesinthestates.com | datesinthestatesblog@gmail.com |

Sponsors & Affiliates

Our sponsors and affiliates help make our adventures possible! Explore the amazing brands and businesses that support our community.

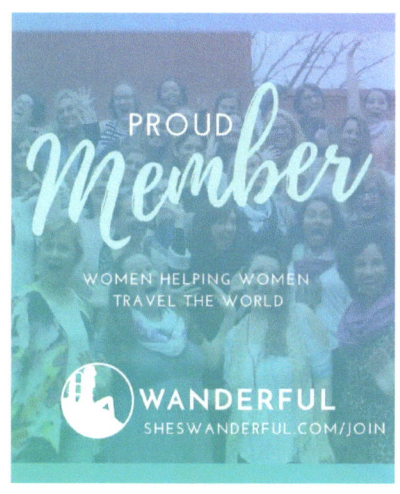

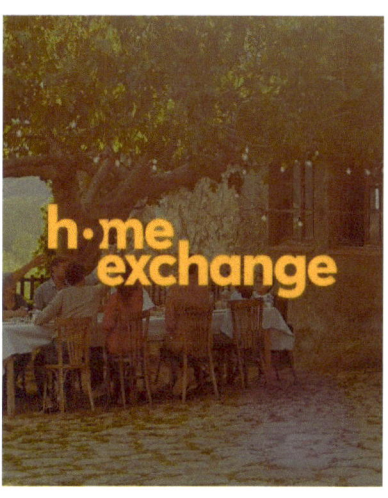

Wanderful

Wanderful is a global community for women who love to travel. Connect, explore, and join a local hub near you!

Join our Book Club!

Join our Mystery Date Book Club and be part of a travel-inspired community, discovering unique local adventures together!

HomeExchange

HomeExchange lets you swap homes with travelers worldwide for authentic, affordable stays. Join today and travel differently!

Shop our books at a store near you!

Little Button Craft
658 South Ave.
Rochester, NY 14620

The Pawsitive Cat Cafe
120 East Ave. Ste 100
Rochester, NY 14604

Yesterday's Muse Books
32 West Main St.
Webster, NY 14580

Writers & Books
740 University Ave,
Rochester, NY 14607

Littleberger Florist
63 North Avenue,
Webster, NY 14580

Flight Wine Bar
262 Exchange Blvd,
Rochester, NY 14608

Scents by Design
728 University Ave,
Rochester, NY 14607

Union Tavern
4565 Culver Rd,
Irondequoit, NY 14622

DATES IN THE STATES

A COUPLE TRAVELING THE UNITED
STATES ON A BUDGET

Contact Us

datesinthestates.com

datesinthestatesblog@gmail.com

Based in Rochester, NY

CONNECT WITH US ON SOCIAL!

@DATESINTHESTATES